CODING
STEM

TRANSPORT

Real-world coding projects made fun

**Max
Wainewright**

WAYLAND
www.waylandbooks.co.uk

Published in paperback in Great Britain in 2020 by Wayland

Text copyright © ICT Apps, 2019
Art and design copyright © Hodder and Stoughton, 2019

Credits:
Editor: Elise Short
Designer: Peter Scoulding
Cover Design: Peter Scoulding
Illustrations: John Haslam

Every attempt has been made to clear copyright. Should there be any inadvertent omission please apply to the publisher for rectification.

ISBN: 978 1 5263 0878 8

Printed and bound in China

Picture credits:

Shutterstock: Ryan Fletcher 6, Sergey Zaykov 10, Sanit Fuangnakhon 12, Oleksiy Mark 15, metamorworks 18, Zapp2Photo 23, FamVeld 24, Lenscap Photography 27, Alamy Stock Photo: SiliconValleyStock 20.

Wayland, an imprint of
Hachette Children's Group
Part of Hodder and Stoughton
Carmelite House
50 Victoria Embankment
London EC4Y 0DZ

An Hachette UK Company
www.hachette.co.uk
www.hachettechildrens.co.uk

We recommend that children are supervised at all times when using the internet. Some of the projects in this series require the use a computer webcam and microphone. Please make sure children are made aware that they should only allow a computer to access the webcam or microphone on specific websites that a trusted adult has told them to use. We do not recommend children use webcams or microphones on any other websites other than those mentioned in this book.

The website addresses (URLs) included in this book were valid at the time of going to press. However, it is possible that contents or addresses may have changed since the publication of this book. No responsibility for any such changes can be accepted by either the author or the Publisher.

Scratch is developed by the Lifelong Kindergarten Group at the MIT Media Lab. See http://scratch.mit.edu. Images and illustrations from Scratch included in this book have been developed by the Lifelong Kindergarten Group at the MIT Media Lab (see http://scratch.mit.edu) and made available under the Creative Commons Attribution-ShareAlike 2.0 licence (https://creativecommons.org/licenses/by-sa/2.0/deed.en). The third party trademarks used in this book are the property of their respective owners, including the Scratch name and logo. The owners of these trademarks have not endorsed, authorised or sponsored this book.

Contents

Introduction

In this book you will learn how technology is used in some modern vehicles. You'll find out how computer technology is changing traditional forms of transport, and enabling brand new forms to be invented.

We'll spend some time looking at how the technology works in various types of transport, learning about the different parts of each system. Alongside that we will have a look inside the computer code that connects up the components and brings things to life.

You'll use the algorithms and ideas that control real forms of transport technology to create your own programs. These programs will help you understand how things work – and set you on the road to dreaming up your own ideas for the future of transport!

There are lots of different ways to create code. We will be using a website called Scratch to do our coding.

Type **scratch.mit.edu** into your web browser, then click Create to start a new project.

Let's start by looking at the important parts of the screen in Scratch:

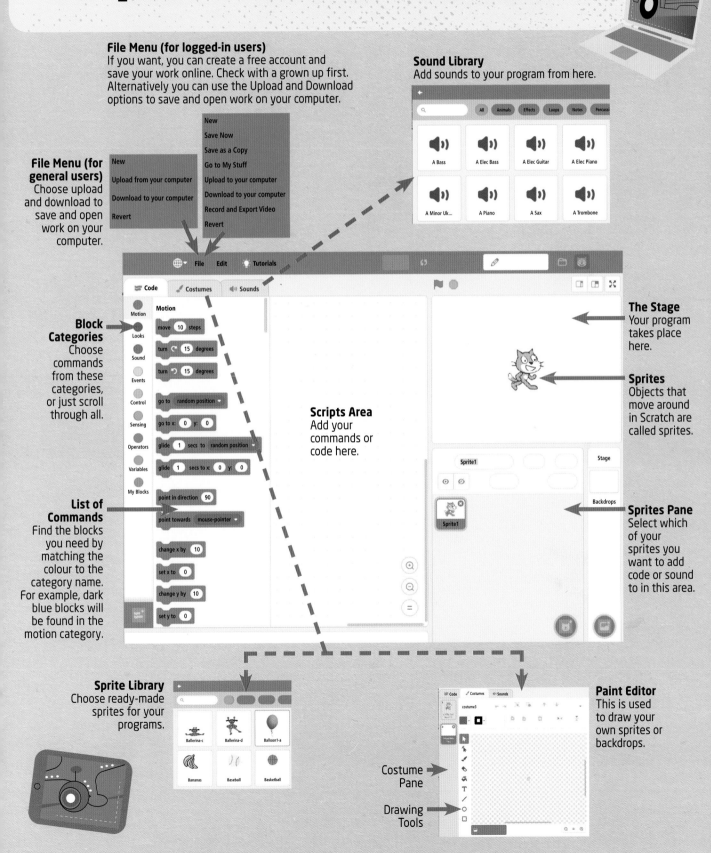

File Menu (for logged-in users)
If you want, you can create a free account and save your work online. Check with a grown up first. Alternatively you can use the Upload and Download options to save and open work on your computer.

Sound Library
Add sounds to your program from here.

File Menu (for general users)
Choose upload and download to save and open work on your computer.

New
Upload from your computer
Download to your computer
Revert

New
Save Now
Save as a Copy
Go to My Stuff
Upload to your computer
Download to your computer
Record and Export Video
Revert

Block Categories
Choose commands from these categories, or just scroll through all.

The Stage
Your program takes place here.

Sprites
Objects that move around in Scratch are called sprites.

Scripts Area
Add your commands or code here.

List of Commands
Find the blocks you need by matching the colour to the category name. For example, dark blue blocks will be found in the motion category.

Sprites Pane
Select which of your sprites you want to add code or sound to in this area.

Sprite Library
Choose ready-made sprites for your programs.

Paint Editor
This is used to draw your own sprites or backdrops.

Costume Pane

Drawing Tools

Automotive Technology

The first cars were on the road over 130 years ago. These early cars were much simpler than today's vehicles.

Over time electronics and computers started to play a bigger role in cars. Computers now control how the different components of a car are connected together. Cables and levers are being replaced by electronic switches, wires, computers and special motors called servos. **Let's build our own car with code to see how these systems work.**

STEP 1 - Remove the cat

Right-click the cat sprite and click **delete**.

STEP 2 - Add a sprite

Hover over the **Choose sprite** button.

Click the **brush** icon.

STEP 3 - Start drawing

Click **Convert to Bitmap**.

Select the **Rectangle** tool.

Choose a colour for your car.

Set the rectangle to **Filled**.

STEP 4 - Draw the car

Start by drawing a rectangle. Make it about ¾ of the width of the Drawing Area.

Click the **Line** tool.

Make the line thicker.

Draw the windscreen.

Add a roof.

Draw the boot ...

... and the pillars.

STEP 5 - Final details

Add any other details with a thinner line in a darker colour.

Click the **Undo** tool if you make a mistake.

Round the corners off with the **Rubber**.

For help go to: www.maxw.com

Hold down the shift key to make an exact circle.

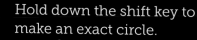

STEP 6 - Draw a wheel

Hover over the **Choose a Sprite** button.

Click the **Brush** icon.

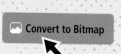

Click **Convert to Bitmap**.

Choose black.

Now click the **Ellipse** tool.

Draw the tyre.

Choose grey.

Draw the wheel inside the tyre.

Drag the wheel so it's in the middle of the tyre.

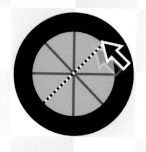

Use the Zoom controls to get a better view when adding small details.

Use the **Line** tool to draw dark grey spoke details on the wheel.

STEP 7 - Get coding

First we need to make a variable that can store the speed of the car:

Click the **Code** tab.

Click the **Variables** category.

Click **Make a Variable**.

Type **speed**.

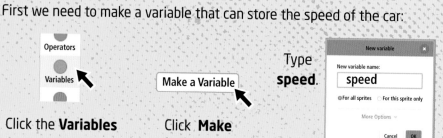

New variable

New variable name:

    speed

○ For all sprites   ○ For this sprite only

More Options ▾

Cancel   OK

Click **OK**.

Now drag these code blocks into the script area.

Use the colours to help you find the correct group for each block.

See page 30 for help positioning blocks.

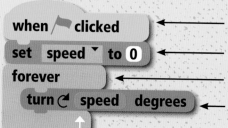

when ⚑ clicked

set speed ▾ to 0

forever

    turn ↻ speed degrees

Run this code when the green flag is clicked:

Set the speed to zero.

Keep looping this code forever:

Rotate the wheels according to the size of the speed variable.

8

The Accelerator

How it works

When driving a car you need to control how fast it is going. You do this with the accelerator pedal. In traditional petrol-powered cars the throttle cable connects the pedal to the engine. Pressing the pedal harder sends more air and petrol to the engine, making the engine turn faster. This then makes the wheels turn faster and the car accelerates.

In an electric car the pedal is connected to a computer. A sensor on the pedal tells the computer how far it is pressed. The computer then delivers the correct amount of energy from the battery to one or more electric motors. The motors then drive the wheels round faster.

For our car we have simplified things. Instead of a pedal we will use a slider to change the speed.

STEP 8 - Position the front wheel

We need to move the wheel into the correct position, and set the centre so it spins smoothly.

Click the **Costumes** tab.	Choose the **Select** tool.	Draw around the wheel to select it.	Drag the wheel to the centre of the Drawing Area.	Now over on the Stage, drag the wheel to the front of the car.

STEP 9 - Let's go!

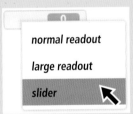

Find the speed variable in the top left corner of the screen. Hover over it and click the right mouse button. Then choose 'slider'.

Click the flag.

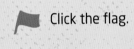

Gradually drag the slider to the right to set the speed, and watch what happens!

STEP 10 - Back wheel

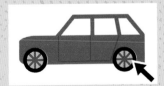

Right-click the **wheel sprite**.

Click **duplicate**.

Drag the new wheel to the back.

 Click the flag and test your code again, by moving the slider.

STEP 11 - Find sound FX

Start by finding a sound for the horn.

Click **Sprite1** (the car sprite) in the **Sprites pane**.

Click the **Sounds** tab.

Click the **Choose a Sound** icon.

Click **C2 trombone**.

STEP 12 - Sound the horn

Most cars have a switch on the steering wheel which sounds the horn. Let's link ours to one of the keys on the keyboard.

Now click the **Code** tab and drag in this code:

Run this code when the h key is pressed down. (Choose h from the drop down.)

Play the horn sound effect.

 Click the flag. Now try pressing the h key on the keyboard.

Indicators are used to warn other road users when a car is about to change direction. Over time these have evolved from a mechanical flipper to the flashing orange lights we have today. To make our lights flash we will use code to hide and show them.

STEP 13 - Add indicators

Hover over the **Choose a Sprite** button.

Click the **Brush** icon.

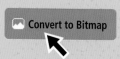

Click **Convert to Bitmap**.

Select the **Rectangle** tool.

Choose orange.

STEP 14 - Draw the indicators

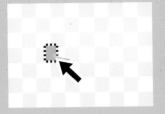

Draw a small rectangle.

Round the corners off with the **Rubber**.

Now drag it into place on the car.

STEP 15 - Flashing code

Click the **Code** tab and drag in this code to make it flash when the **i key** is pressed:

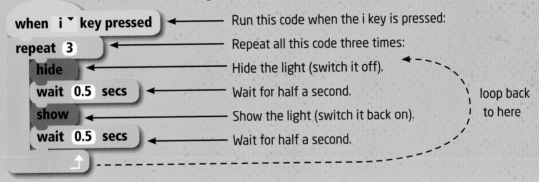

when i ▾ key pressed ← Run this code when the i key is pressed:

repeat 3 ← Repeat all this code three times:

hide ← Hide the light (switch it off).

wait 0.5 secs ← Wait for half a second.

show ← Show the light (switch it back on).

wait 0.5 secs ← Wait for half a second.

loop back to here

Investigate

In the flashing code, try changing the number 3 at the top of the repeat block.

What happens if you change the number of seconds in the wait command?

Code challenge

Add a second indicator light to the back of the car.

When it gets dark the car will need headlights. They won't need to flash. Make them come on when you press one key, and turn off when you press another.

How about adding a radio or MP3 player to your car? Make it play one of the **musical loops** in the sounds tab when a key is pressed on the keyboard.

What else can you add to your car?

Drones

A drone is a flying machine similar to a helicopter – but with no pilot! Most drones are flown by remote control, with a human controlling where the drone goes.

Drones that are controlled entirely by computers are now being developed. A human tells the computer where the drone needs to go, such as an address to deliver a parcel, and the drone works out how to get there! **Let's have a look at how they work and build our own on-screen drone with code.**

STEP 1 - Remove the cat

Right-click the cat sprite and click **delete**.

duplicate
delete
export

STEP 2 - Add a sprite

 Hover over the **Choose a Sprite** button.

 Click the **Brush** icon.

For help go to:
www.maxw.com

STEP 3 - Draw the frame

Click **Convert to Bitmap**.

Select the **Line** tool.

Choose a colour for the drone.

Make the line thicker.

Start the frame with a line.

Add a second line.

Choose **Rectangle** and select **Filled**. Complete the drone frame.

STEP 4 - Add the propellor

Hover over the **Choose a Sprite** button.

Click the **Brush** icon.

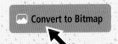

Click **Convert to Bitmap**.

Select the **Ellipse** tool.

Choose a colour.

Draw a small, thin oval in the centre of the Drawing Area.

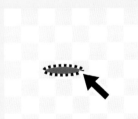

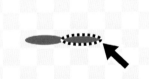

Add a second oval to complete the propellor.

STEP 5 - Position the propellor

Choose the **Select** tool.

Draw around the propellor to select it.

Drag it to the centre of the Drawing Area.

On the Stage, drag the propellor to one edge of the drone's frame.

STEP 6 - Get coding

We need a variable that can store the speed of the propellor.

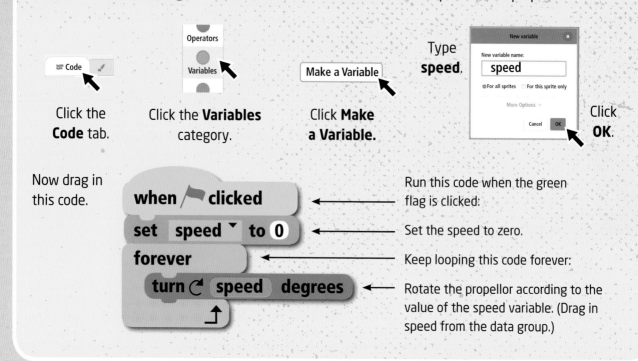

Click the **Code** tab.

Click the **Variables** category.

Click **Make a Variable.**

Type **speed**.

Click **OK**.

Now drag in this code.

Run this code when the green flag is clicked:

Set the speed to zero.

Keep looping this code forever:

Rotate the propellor according to the value of the speed variable. (Drag in speed from the data group.)

STEP 7 - Take off!

Find the speed variable in the top left corner of the screen. Hover over it and click right. Then choose **slider**.

Click the flag.

Gradually drag the slider to the right to set the speed of the propellor.

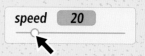

STEP 8 - More propellors

Right-click the **propellor sprite**.

Click **duplicate**.

Drag the new propellor into the corner opposite the first one.

OCATIO**N** TO:−

ard

E OUT OF — TRANSIT

REFRES **F 1**

R SUBJE **C T**

AUTH **O R**

ON CHE **C K**

CK

ATION

ATION

propri **a te)**

Let's make the new propellor green, to differentiate it:

Click the **Costumes** tab.

Select green, then use the **Fill** tool to recolour it.

Repeat step 6 to duplicate the final propellor.

Your drone should now look like this. Use the green flag to run your code, and the slider to control the speed of the propellors. Notice the direction each propellor rotates.

How it works

Frame
All the components are attached to a frame or chassis.

Legs
To land on.

Camera
Most drones either carry a camera or some kind of load (such as a parcel for delivery).

Computer
A computer controls all the different systems within the drone.

GPS
A GPS system may be added to detect the drone's location and determine its height in relation to the ground.

Four motors and propellors
The speed of each motor is controlled by the computer. Changing the speed of different pairs of motors makes the drone move forwards, backwards, or rotate. Making all the motors change speed causes the drone to go up or down.

Gyro
A gyroscope ('Gyro') is located inside the drone. This is used to keep the drone stable.

Destination Drone

Now we know how drones fly, let's program a drone to make it reach a particular destination. Save your old progam and start a new file in Scratch.

STEP 1 - Remove the cat

Right-click the cat sprite and click **delete**.

STEP 2 - Add a sprite

Hover over the **Choose a Sprite** button.

Click the **Brush** icon.

STEP 3 - Draw a drone from the side

Click **Convert to Bitmap**.

Select the **Rectangle** tool.

Choose a colour for your drone.

Set the rectangle to **Filled**.

Draw a thin rectangle about half the width of the Drawing Area.

Click the **Ellipse** tool.

Draw a circle to house the computer and drone systems.

Add a small circle at each edge of the drone for the motors.

STEP 4 - Duplicate your costume

To make it look as though the propellors are rotating, let's create a two-frame animation. We will need a second frame or 'costume' for the sprite to do this. This is done by duplicating what you have just drawn.

Find **costume1** in the top left of the screen, and right-click it.

Click **duplicate**.

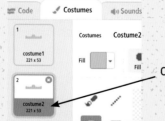

The second costume will be shown here.

For help go to: www.maxw.com

STEP 5 - Costume 2

Use the **Ellipse** tool to add a green propellor blade on the left side, and a red one on the right.

STEP 6 - Costume 1

Now switch back to **costume1**.

Draw the two propellors again, but in different positions.

STEP 7 - Add code to make it fly!

Click the **Code** tab and drag in this code:

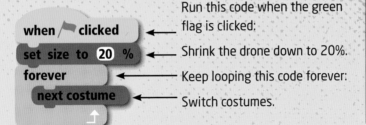

Run this code when the green flag is clicked:

Shrink the drone down to 20%.

Keep looping this code forever:

Switch costumes.

This section of code will keep swapping over the two sprite costumes, giving the illusion that the propellors are rotating.

Now add this second section of code.

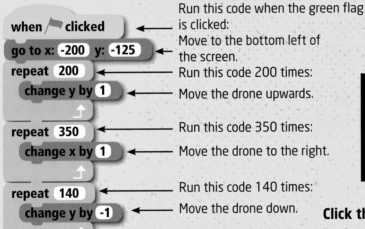

Run this code when the green flag is clicked:
Move to the bottom left of the screen.

Run this code 200 times:
Move the drone upwards.

Run this code 350 times:
Move the drone to the right.

Run this code 140 times:
Move the drone down.

This part of the code controls the path that the drone will take on its journey.

Click the flag to test your code.

Investigate

Change the values at the start of the **Repeat** blocks. What happens?

In the **change x** and **y** blocks try swapping the 1 and -1 around. See what difference it makes.

Code challenge

Click on the **Stage** icon in the **Sprites pane**, at the bottom left of the screen. Go to the Drawing Area and click on **Backdrops**. Try drawing a background of a city.

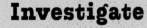

Now change the second section of code to make the drone take off from one building in the city and land on the other side. (As you move your mouse you will see the x and y co-ordinates displayed on the right below the Stage. Use the values to help you.)

Self-Driving Cars

We've already looked at how transport technology has become more and more sophisticated. Many new cars today have computers that can help the driver. These include sensors to check if the car is too close to another, or if it is not staying in its lane on a motorway.

A few cars have computers that can go much further and actually drive themselves for part of the journey. Not everyone thinks this is a good idea – will self-driving cars be better drivers than humans? How does the technology work? **Let's find out by coding our own self-driving car.**

STEP 1 - Remove the cat

Right-click the cat sprite and click **delete**.

STEP 2 - Add a sprite

Hover over the **Choose a Sprite** button.

Click the **Brush** icon.

Now draw your futuristic car. Make sure you show it in **plan view** – drawn from above.

STEP 3 - Start drawing

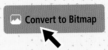

Click **Convert to Bitmap**.

Select the **Rectangle** tool.

Choose a colour for your car.

Set the rectangle to **Filled**.

STEP 4 - Draw the car

Start by drawing a rectangle. Make it about half the width of the Drawing Area.

Now click the **Ellipse** tool.

Draw an ellipse to make the front of the car curvy, and drag it into place.

STEP 5 - Add a windscreen

Choose light grey for the glass.

Draw the windscreen.

Go back to the colour you chose for the body.

Draw the roof.

STEP 6 - Wheel arches and final details

Draw four wheel arches to make the car look more powerful and streamlined.

Maybe add some stripes with the line tool!

For help go to: www.maxw.com

19

STEP 7 - Get moving

Click the **Code** tab and drag in this code:

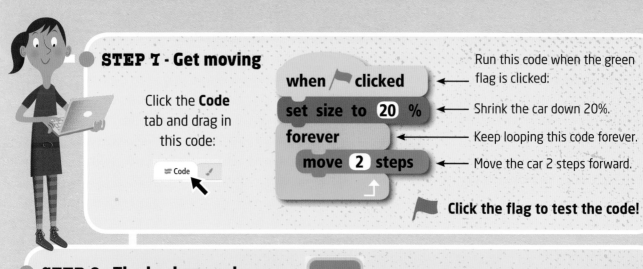

Run this code when the green flag is clicked:

← Shrink the car down 20%.

← Keep looping this code forever.

← Move the car 2 steps forward.

Click the flag to test the code!

STEP 8 - The background

Click on the **Stage** icon next to the Sprites pane.

Click the **Backdrops** tab.

STEP 9 - Draw a road

Click **Convert to Bitmap**.

Use the **Brush** tool.

Pick dark grey.

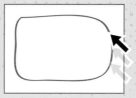

Draw the edge of a large road. It should fill most of the space.

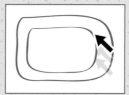

Now draw the inside edge of the road. Make sure there are no gaps.

Fill the gap to make a thick grey road.

↺ *If the colour leaks out click undo and fill up any gaps with the brush. Then try filling it again.*

To keep the car on the road we need to find a way for it to detect where the road is. Self-driving cars use sensors to do this.

Google have built a self-driving car. To detect obstacles it has a laser scanner and radar system on top of its roof. The scanner rotates to check all around the car.

We will add a sensor on the left-hand side of the car. This will check if the car is near the left side of the road.

STEP 10 - Add a sensor

Select the **car sprite**.

Pick the **Rectangle** tool.

Choose red.

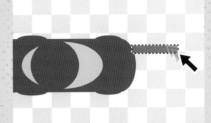

Drag out a long, thin rectangle to be the sensor beam. Make sure it looks like this.

If the car senses an obstacle on its left, or the left side of the road, then it needs to move away from it, by turning right.

STEP 11 - Turn right

Click the **Code** tab and change your code so it looks like this:

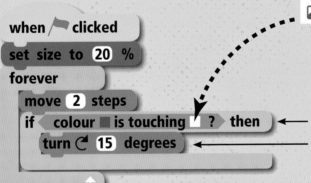

```
when 🏳 clicked
set size to 20 %
forever
    move 2 steps
    if   colour ■ is touching □ ? then
        turn ↻ 15 degrees
```

Set these colours by clicking inside the square, then clicking the pipette and clicking on a colour from the Stage.

Check if the red sensor beam is touching white (off the road).

If so, turn right 15 degrees.

🚩 **Click the flag to test the code!**

How it works:

1. To start, the loop keeps the car moving in a straight line.

3. ... the car starts to turn to the right.

2. When the sensor beam detects that the edge of the road is ahead ...

Real roads turn left and right. We're going to change our road and add another sensor.

STEP 12 - Curve test

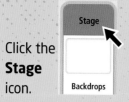

Click the **Stage** icon.

Choose the **Backdrops** tab.

Hover over the **Choose a Backdrop** button.

Paint

Click the **Brush** icon.

Click **Convert to Bitmap**.

Choose the **Brush** tool.

Pick dark grey.

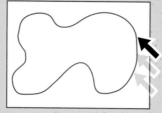

Draw a new road. Give it lots of bends. Avoid tight corners.

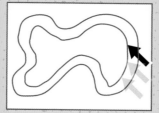

Now draw the inside of the road. Make sure there are no gaps.

Fill the gap to make a thick grey road.

STEP 13 - Second sensor

Select the **car sprite**.

Pick the **Rectangle** tool.

Choose orange.

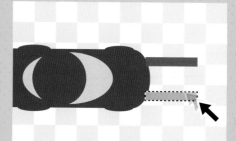

Draw an orange rectangle below the red one. This will be our second sensor beam.

STEP 14 - Code upgrade

We need to upgrade our code to include the new orange sensor beam. If it touches the edge of the road, the car needs to turn left.

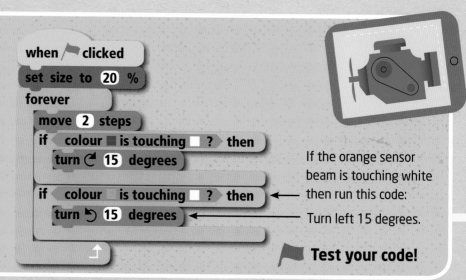

```
when 🏴 clicked
set size to 20 %
forever
    move 2 steps
    if  colour ■ is touching □ ? then
        turn ↻ 15 degrees

    if  colour ■ is touching □ ? then
        turn ↺ 15 degrees
```

If the orange sensor beam is touching white then run this code:

Turn left 15 degrees.

🏴 **Test your code!**

Investigate

Code challenge

What happens if you change the width and length of the red and orange sensor beams?

At the moment the car turns 15 degrees when it detects an obstacle. Try changing this value - does this make the car better or worse at driving?

Some self-driving cars only work at slow speed. Our car moves 2 steps every time the loop runs. If we increase this value does the car become dangerous? Experiment to find the fastest safe speed it can travel around your road.

Add a second car by duplicating it, and its code. How about a third or fourth car?

Make each car travel at a different speed.

Add more code so the cars avoid each other. You might need to add another sensor to do this. It could make the cars stop, slow down or move back if they detect another car nearby.

Sensors

How do they work?

If you shout out "Hello" in the middle of an empty field you won't hear anything. But try shouting inside a tunnel and you will hear an echo. This is caused by the sound bouncing back off the walls of the tunnel.

Real sensors and radar systems work in the same way. They send out a radio wave (radar) or an infared beam of radiation (sensor). If there are any obtacles nearby then part of the beam will bounce back.

If the object is nearby then it will bounce back quickly. Sensors measure how long it takes the beam to bounce back and use this value to calculate how far away the obstacle is.

The Google self-driving car has no steering wheel, accelerator or brake. It does have sensors, but the car is a little more sophisticated than the one we coded. It uses cameras as well as sensors. They are combined to work out where obstacles are.

The car uses AI (Artificial Intelligence) software to work out what the obstacles are. The software analyses the size, speed and the way the obstacle moves. It then works out whether the obstacle is another car, bike or pedestrian, and what it should do.

Self-driving cars also use GPS technology to work out where they are - they don't want to get lost any more than human drivers do!

Hoverboard Scooters

Hoverboard scooters are a brand new form of transport made possible by new technology. The board doesn't actually hover but a computer helps riders balance on just two wheels.

The rider moves and steers the hoverboard by leaning and pressing down on switches with their feet. **Let's find out how they work by building our own with code.**

STEP 1 - Remove the cat

Right-click the cat sprite and click **delete**.

STEP 2 - The background

Click the **Backdrops** tab.

For help go to:
www.maxw.com

STEP 3 - Start drawing

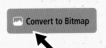

Click **Convert to Bitmap**.

Choose the **Rectangle** tool.

Pick **Filled** then choose a colour.

Draw a very large, pale blue rectangle for the sky.

Add a second brown rectangle to be the ground.

Draw a third thin green rectangle to be the grass.

STEP 4 - Add a sprite

Hover over the **Choose sprite** button.

Click the **brush** icon.

STEP 5 - We need wheels

Click **Convert to Bitmap**.

Now click the **Ellipse** tool.

Choose black.

Draw the tyre in the centre of the Drawing Area.

Add a grey wheel in the centre of the tyre.

STEP 6 - The rider

Select the **Rectangle** tool and choose a colour.

Draw the rider's legs.

Then add their body.

Click the **Ellipse** tool, then pick a skin colour.

Draw their head.

STEP 7 - Final details

Choose the **Line** tool and pick a colour.

Make the line fairly thick.

Draw their arms.

Pick the **Brush** tool.

Add any final details.

STEP 8 - Start coding

We need a variable that can store the angle of the hoverboard.

Click the **Code** tab.

Click the **Variables** category.

Click **Make a Variable.**

Type **angle**.

Click **OK**.

STEP 9 - The main code

Drag in this code.

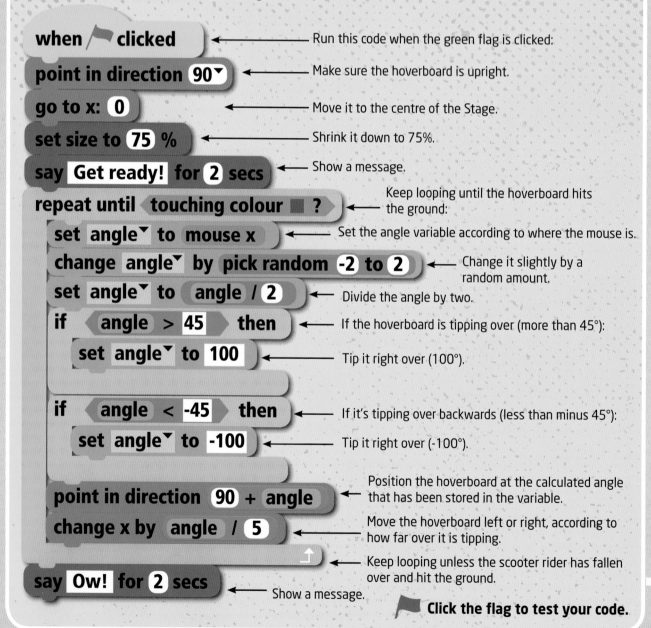

when ⚑ clicked ← Run this code when the green flag is clicked:

point in direction 90▾ ← Make sure the hoverboard is upright.

go to x: 0 ← Move it to the centre of the Stage.

set size to 75 % ← Shrink it down to 75%.

say Get ready! for 2 secs ← Show a message.

repeat until touching colour ■ ? ← Keep looping until the hoverboard hits the ground:

set angle▾ to mouse x ← Set the angle variable according to where the mouse is.

change angle▾ by pick random -2 to 2 ← Change it slightly by a random amount.

set angle▾ to angle / 2 ← Divide the angle by two.

if angle > 45 then ← If the hoverboard is tipping over (more than 45°):

set angle▾ to 100 ← Tip it right over (100°).

if angle < -45 then ← If it's tipping over backwards (less than minus 45°):

set angle▾ to -100 ← Tip it right over (-100°).

point in direction 90 + angle ← Position the hoverboard at the calculated angle that has been stored in the variable.

change x by angle / 5 ← Move the hoverboard left or right, according to how far over it is tipping.

↻ ← Keep looping unless the scooter rider has fallen over and hit the ground.

say Ow! for 2 secs ← Show a message.

⚑ **Click the flag to test your code.**

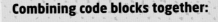

Here are some tips to help you put the code on the left together:

Setting the touching colour code block:

touching colour

First click the colour selector square.

Next click the pipette, then click on a colour somewhere on the Stage.

Using random numbers:

pick random -2 to 2

Drag the **pick random** block into your code. Type in two numbers. The first one sets the smallest number you need, the second the largest. When the code runs it will pick one for you.

Combining code blocks together:

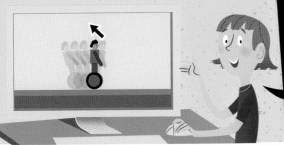

set angle▾ to 0

Start by dragging in a **set angle** block.

set angle▾ to ◯ / ◯

Next drag in a **division** block from the **Operators** group.

set angle▾ to ◯ / angle

From the **Data** group drag in an **angle** block.

set angle▾ to angle / 2

Type a 2 inside the **division** block.

Drag your scooter down so the wheels are touching the top of the grass. Use your mouse to balance your hoverboard. Move the mouse gently to the left or right of the screen to adjust your balance. Make sure your mouse pointer is in the middle of the screen when you start.

How it works

Steering
There is no steering wheel on a hoverboard. You steer by pushing or leaning further on one foot. For example pushing down harder on the right foot makes the motor on the right side go faster, turning the board to the left.

Wheels
There is a wheel on each side of the board.

Motors
Inside the board are two motors, one attached to each wheel.

Pivot
The hoverboard frame has two halves, which are joined in the middle by a pivot. This allows the rider to balance on each leg more easily.

Sensors
Special gyroscopes and sensors are used to measure how fast the wheels are turning and the angle of each half of the board.

Switches
The rider places each foot on a pedal. There are switches underneath the pedals. Leaning gently forwards or backwards activates the switches and tells the hoverboard to move.

Computer
An onboard computer reads data from the sensors and switches. It uses this information to decide how much power to send to each motor.

Hoverboard Game

Let's use our hoverboard scooter to make a catching game! Drive your scooter backwards and forwards to catch all the apples and score points.

Score: 7

STEP 1 - Before you start

Make sure you have all the code from the previous two pages in your computer and that your hoverboard works properly on screen.

STEP 2 - Adding an apple

Click the **Choose a Sprite** button.

Apple

Choose the **Apple** sprite.

STEP 3 - The score
Make a variable that can store the score in the game.

Click the **Code** tab.

Click the **Variables** category.

Click **Make a Variable.**

Type **score**.

New variable

New variable name:

score

For all sprites   For this sprite only

More Options

Cancel   OK

Click **OK**.

STEP 4 - Code the apple

Drag in this code to make the apple move:

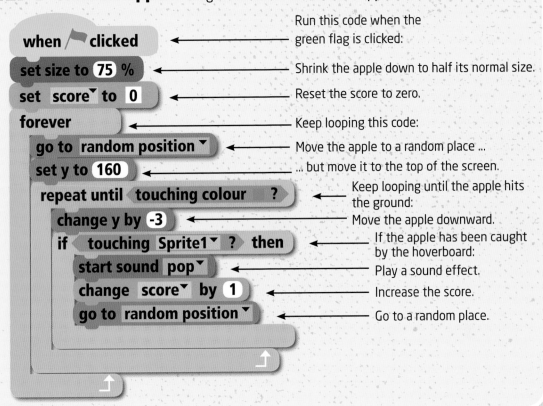

when 🏳 clicked ← Run this code when the green flag is clicked:

set size to (75) % ← Shrink the apple down to half its normal size.

set score▾ to (0) ← Reset the score to zero.

forever ← Keep looping this code:

go to random position▾ ← Move the apple to a random place ...

set y to (160) ← ... but move it to the top of the screen.

repeat until ⟨touching colour (?)⟩ ← Keep looping until the apple hits the ground:

change y by (-3) ← Move the apple downward.

if ⟨touching Sprite1▾ (?)⟩ then ← If the apple has been caught by the hoverboard:

start sound pop▾ ← Play a sound effect.

change score▾ by (1) ← Increase the score.

go to random position▾ ← Go to a random place.

STEP 5 - More apples

Right-click the **apple**.

| duplicate |
| delete |
| export |

Click **duplicate**.

Duplicate the apple again, so you have three apples.

🏳 **Click the flag to test your code.**

Investigate

In the code for the hoverboard scooter, try adjusting the range of the random number that gets picked.

pick random (-5) to (5)

Code challenge

The hoverboard scooter falls over when the angle is more than 45°, or less than minus 45°. Change the code to allow it to tip further over before it falls.

Add a sound effect that is played when the scooter falls over.

Make the apples stop falling when they hit the scooter.

Bugs and Debugging

When you find your code isn't working as expected, stop and look through each command you have put in. Think about what you want it to do, and what it is really telling the computer to do. If you are entering one of the programs in this book, check your have not missed a line. Some things to check:

Joining blocks properly:

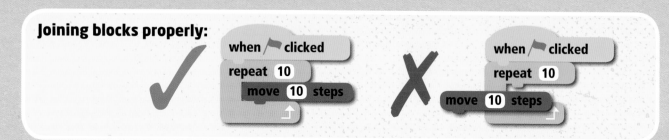

Select sprites before adding code:

Before you add code to a sprite, click on it in the Sprites pane. This will select it and make sure the code is assigned to it. If you don't do this you may find your code is trying to control the wrong sprite!

X or Y?

y Don't mix them up!

The right size

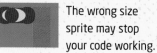

The wrong size sprite may stop your code working. Change the set size per cent value to make them fit properly.

Right colour, wrong code?

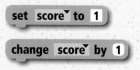

Be precise. Many code blocks look very similar but do completely different things!

Position variables and values carefully

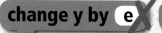

Don't type in variable names.

Don't just drop them on top of blocks.

Drag them until a glowing white circle appears.

The value block will then snap in to place.

Tips to reduce bugs:

• When things aren't working properly, spend time looking through your code so you understand each line. Experiment and change your code, try out different values. To be good at debugging you need to understand what each code block does and how your code works.

• Practise debugging! Make a very short program and get a friend to change one block only while you aren't looking. Can you fix it?

• If you are making your own program, spend time drawing a diagram and planning it before you start. Try changing values if things don't work, and don't be afraid to start again – you will learn from it.

Glossary

AI (artificial intelligence) – software that does more than just follow steps. AI systems respond with apparent intelligence to outside events.

Algorithm – rules or steps followed to make something work or complete a task.

Bug – an error in a program that stops it working properly.

Code block – a draggable instruction icon used in Scratch.

Debug – removing bugs (or errors) from a program.

Degrees – the units used to measure angles.

GPS (Global Positioning System) – a way of finding out exactly where something is, by measuring signals from satellites orbiting the Earth.

Gyro (gyroscope) – a device that can detect the angle it is positioned at, and send this information to a computer.

Hardware – the wires, chips, sensors and physical parts of a system or computer.

Icon – a small clickable image on a computer.

Loop – repeating one or more commands a number of times.

Random – a number that can't be predicted.

Right-click – clicking the right mouse button on a sprite or icon.

Sensor – a device that measures something in the real world, such as how far away an object is, and sends the answer to a computer as a number.

Sequence – commands that are run one after another in order.

Software – a computer program containing instructions written in code.

Sprite – an object with a picture on it that moves around the stage.

Stage – the place in Scratch that sprites move around on.

Steps – small movements made by sprites.

System – a combination of software, hardware, sensors and information.

Variable – part of a program that stores a value that can change. For example the score in a game.

Index

FURTHER INFORMATION

Gifford, Clive. *Get Ahead in Computing* series. Wayland, London, UK: 2017.

Wood, Kevin. *Project Code* series. Franklin Watts, London, UK: 2017

Wainewright, Max. *Generation Code: I'm an Advanced Scratch Coder.* Wayland, London, UK: 2017.